Let's Learn
SPANISH
Coloring Book

Anne-Françoise Hazzan

Minerva Figueroa

PASSPORT BOOKS
NTC/Contemporary Publishing Group

Published by Passport Books,
a division of NTC/Contemporary Publishing Group, Inc.,
4255 West Touhy Avenue,
Lincolnwood (Chicago), Illinois 60712-1975 U.S.A.
© 1986 by NTC/Contemporary Publishing Group, Inc.
Manufactured in the United States of America.
International Standard Book Number: 0-8442-7549-2

0 1 2 3 4 5 6 7 8 9 ML 19 18 17 16 15 14 13

el alfabeto

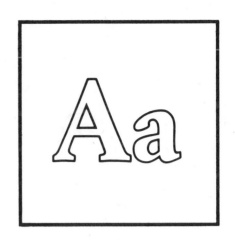

Aa

Aa

los animales

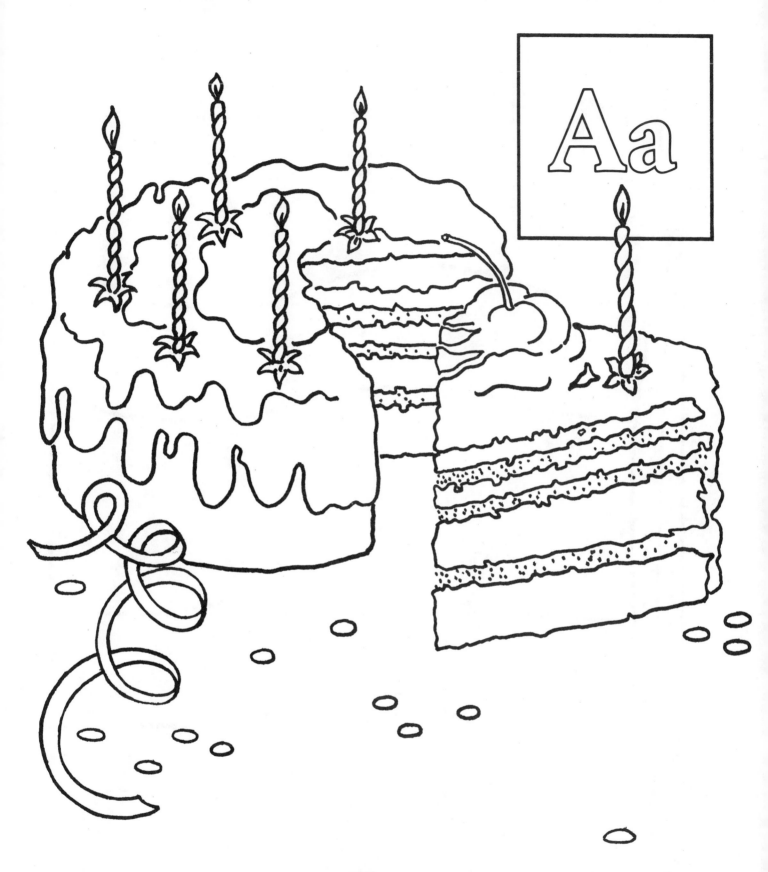

Aa

el aniversario

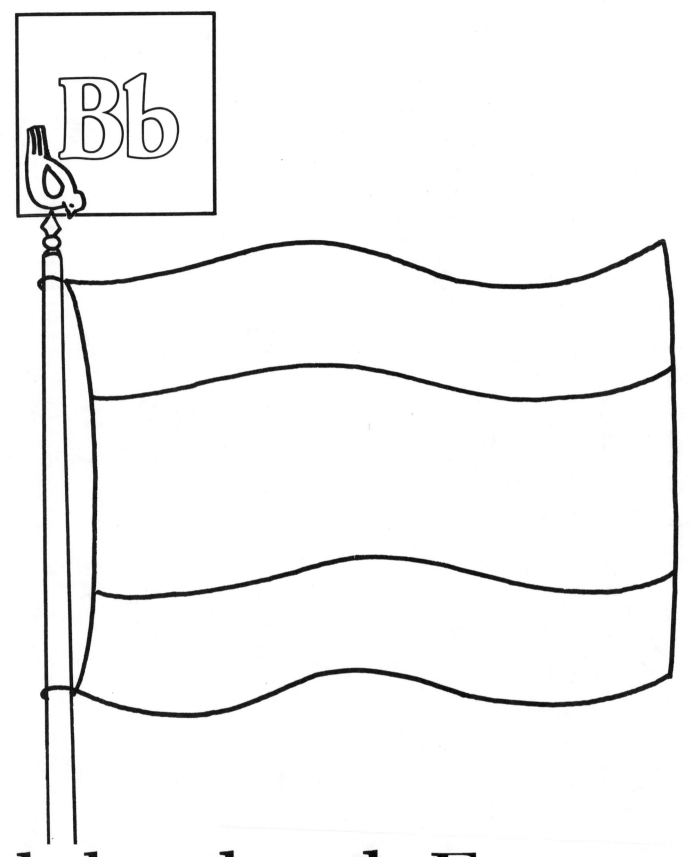

la bandera de España

la bandera de México

Bb

el barco

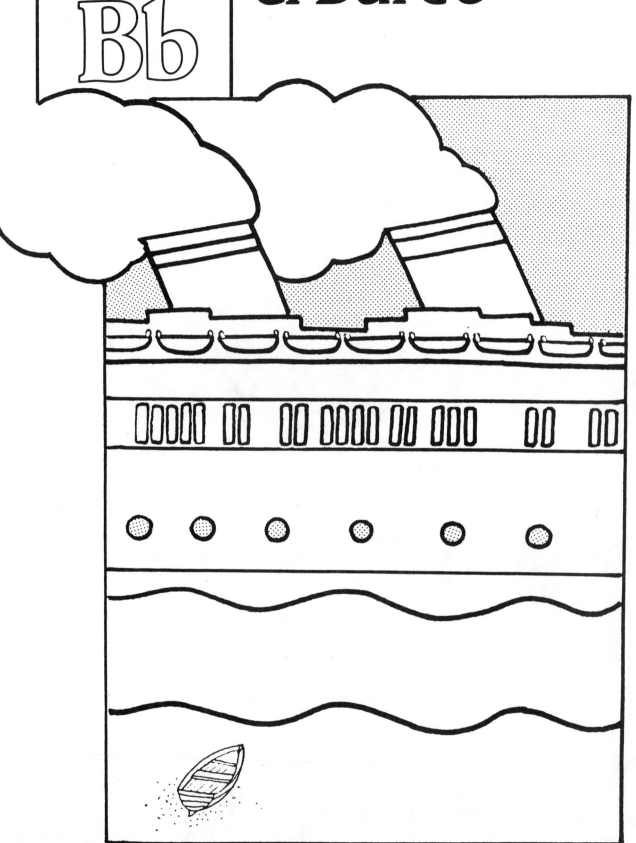

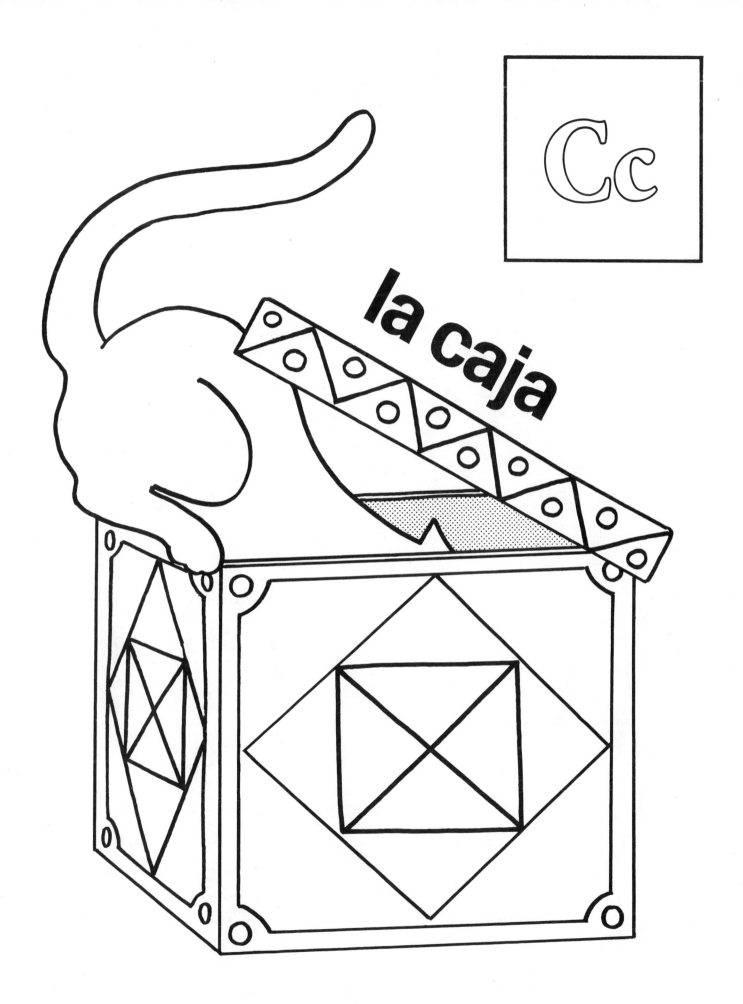

la caja

C c

C c

el canguro

C c

la casa

Ch ch

la chimenea

Ch ch

el chimpancé

la danza

Dd

el dragón

E e

el elefante

E e

España

F f

la familia

la flor

Ff

Ff

las frutas

el gallo

G g

G g

el gato

el ratón

H h

el helado

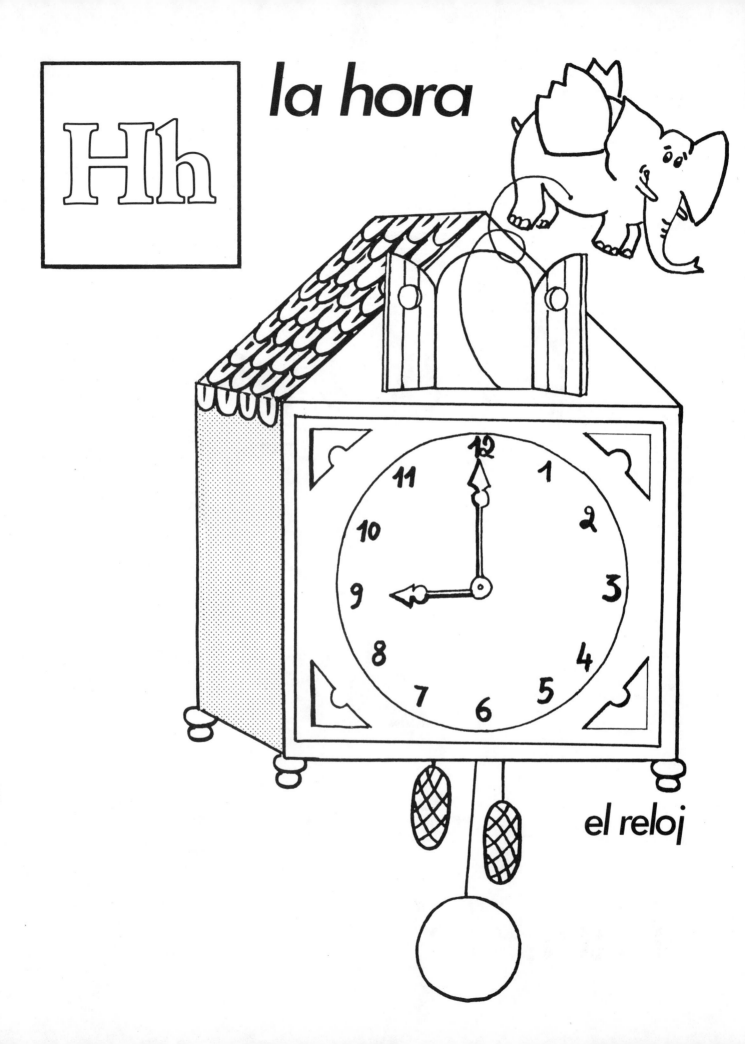

Hh

la hora

el reloj

el invierno

la isla

el jardín

Jj

la zanahoria

el tomate

los juguetes

el kilo

Kk

el pescado

Kk

el kilómetro

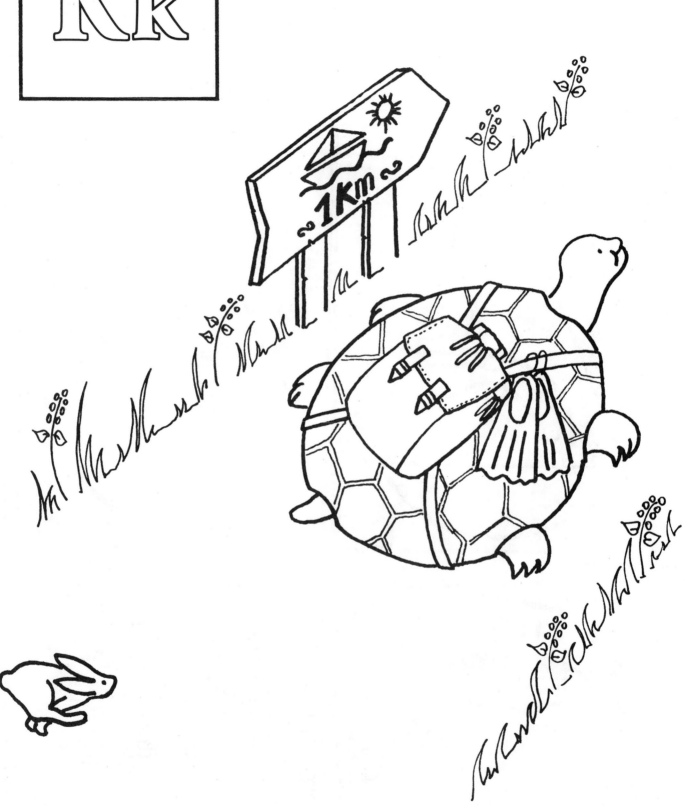

L l

el león

Ll

Gg

el gato

el ratón

Hh

el helado

el libro

la llama

Mm

la mamá

Mm

la mariposa

México

N n

la nieve

la noche

los números

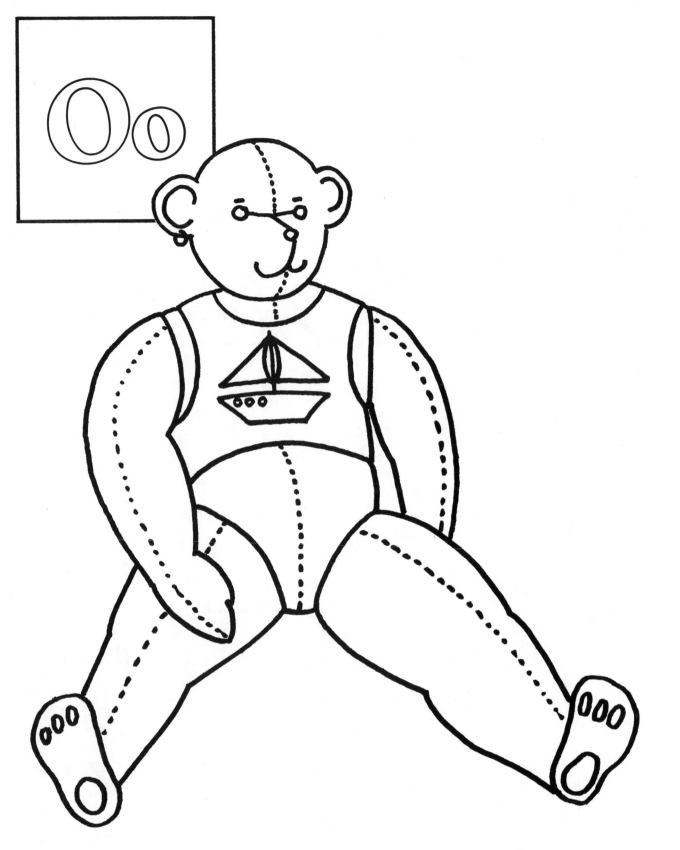

el oso

el otoño

Oo

P p

el pájaro

el papá

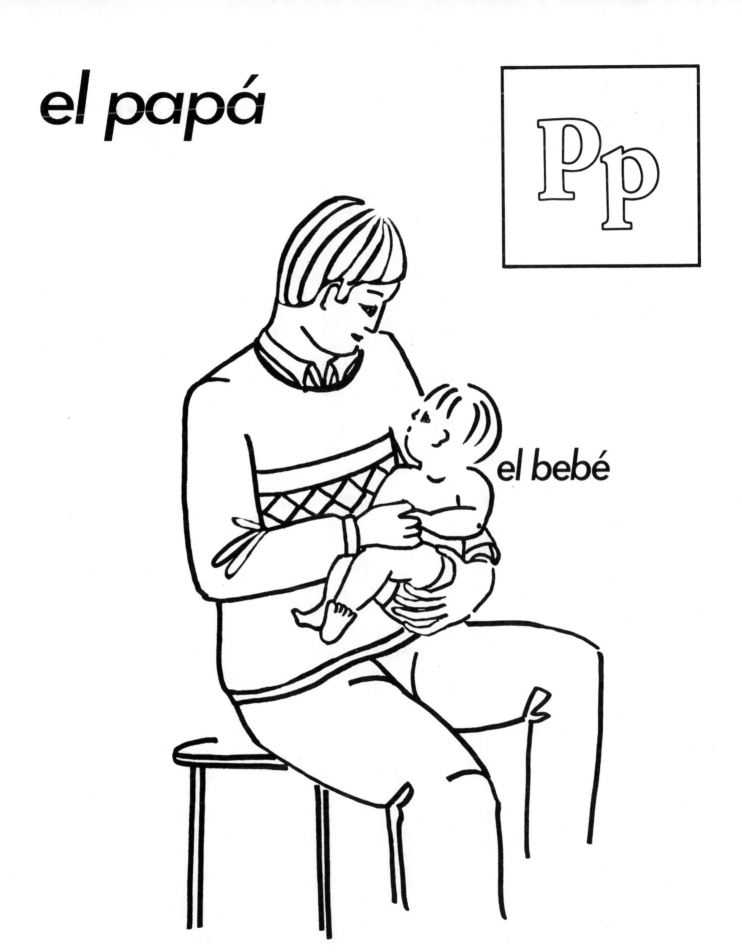

P p

el bebé

P p

la primavera

el queso

R r

el regalo

el rey

la reina

R r

R r

el robot

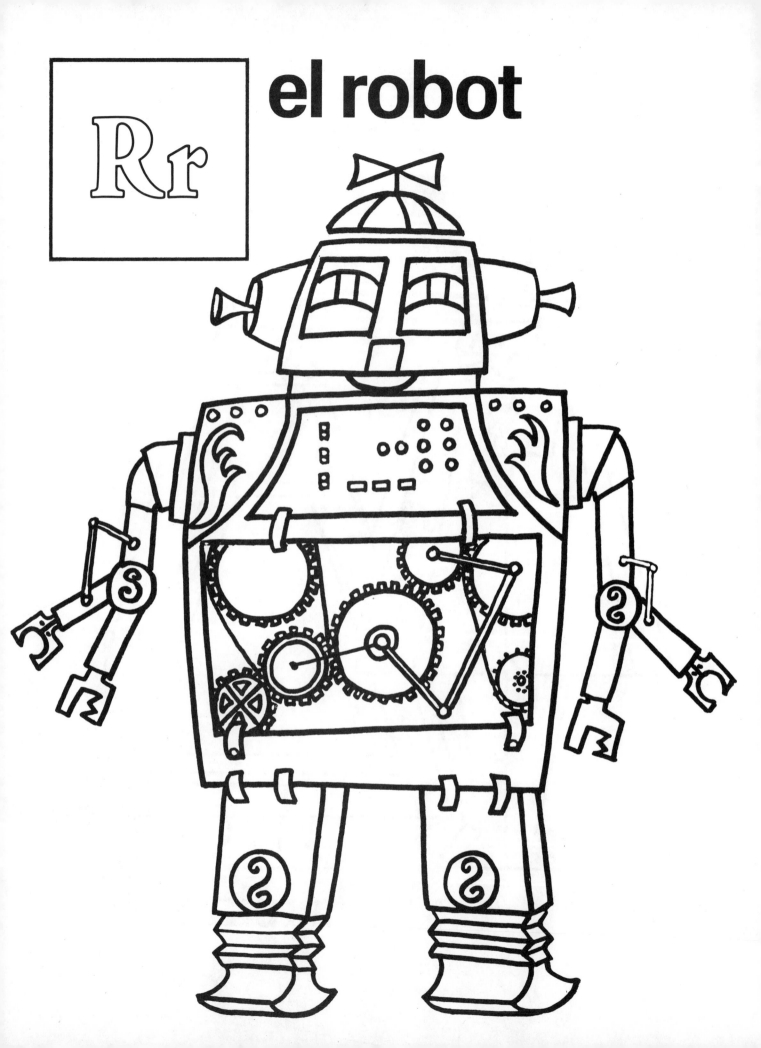

la semana

Ss

lunes

martes

miércoles

jueves

viernes

sábado

domingo

S s

la sirena

Ss

el sol

la luna

S s

el sombrero

el tesoro

Tt

la Tierra

torta
de
frutas

T t

la torta

los uniformes

la ventana

V v

Vv

el verano

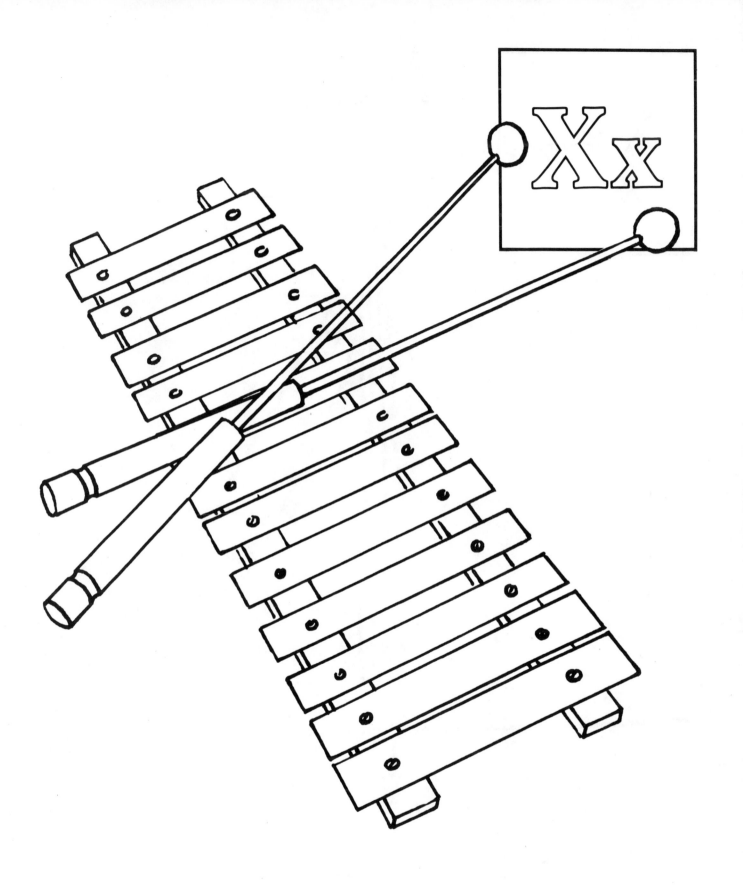

el xilófono

Yy

el yate

Zz

el zorro

Vocabulario

el alfabeto (*m.*) alphabet
el ahl-fah-*bay*-toh

los animales (*m. pl.*) animals
lohs ah-nee-*mah*-lays

el aniversario (*m.*) birthday
el ah-nee-bhayr-*sah*-ree-oh

la bandera (*f.*) flag
lah bahn-*day*-rah

el barco (*m.*) boat
el *bahr*-koh

el bebé (*m.*) baby
el bay-*bay*

la caja (*f.*) box
lah *kah*-hah

el canguro (*m.*) kangaroo
el kahn-*goo*-roh

la casa (*f.*) house
lah *kah*-sah

la chimenea (*f.*) fireplace
lah chee-may-*nay*-ah

el chimpancé (*m.*) chimpanzee
el cheem-pahn-*say*

la danza (*f.*) dance
lah *dahn*-sah

el domingo (*m.*) Sunday
el doh-*meen*-goh

el dragón (*m.*) dragon
el drah-*gohn*

el elefante (*m.*) elephant
el ay-lay-*fahn*-tay

España (*f.*) Spain
ay-*spahn*-yah

la familia (*f.*) family
lah fah-*mee*-lee-ah

la flor (*f.*) flower
lah flohr

las frutas (*f. pl.*) fruit
lahs *froo*-tahs

el gallo (*m.*) rooster
el *gah*-yoh

el gato (*m.*) cat
el *gah*-toh

el helado (*m.*) ice cream
el ay-*lah*-thoh

la hora (*f.*) hour
lah *oh*-rah

el invierno (*m.*) winter
el een-bhee-*ayr*-noh

la isla (*f.*) island
lah *ees*-lah

el jardín (*m.*) garden
el hahr-*deen*

el jueves (*m.*) Thursday
el *hway*-bhays

los juguetes (*m. pl.*) toys
lohs hoo-*gay*-tays

el kilo (*m.*) kilo
el *kee*-loh

el kilómetro (*m.*) kilometer
el kee-*loh*-may-troh

el león (*m.*) lion
el lay-*ohn*

el libro (*m.*) book
el *lee*-broh

la luna (*f.*) moon
lah *loo*-nah

el lunes (*m.*) Monday
el *loo*-nays

la llama (*f.*) llama
lah *yah*-mah

la mamá (*f.*) mother
lah mah-*mah*

la mariposa (*f.*) butterfly
lah mah-ree-*poh*-sah

Vocabulary

el martes (*m.*) Tuesday
el *mahr*-tays

México (*m.*) Mexico
may-hee-koh

el miércoles (*m.*) Wednesday
el mee-*ayr*-koh-lays

la nieve (*f.*) snow
lah nee-*ay*-bhay

la noche (*f.*) night
lah *noh*-chay

los números (*m. pl.*) numbers
lohs *noo*-may-rohs

el oso (*m.*) bear
el *oh*-soh

el otoño (*m.*) autumn, fall
el oh-*tohn*-yoh

el pájaro (*m.*) bird
el *pah*-hah-roh

el papá (*m.*) father
el pah-*pah*

el pescado (*m.*) fish
el pays-*kah*-thoh

la primavera (*f.*) spring
lah pree-mah-*bhay*-rah

el queso (*m.*) cheese
el *kay*-soh

el ratón (*m.*) mouse
el rah-*tohn*

el regalo (*m.*) gift
el ray-*gah*-loh

la reina (*f.*) queen
lah ray-*ee*-nah

el reloj (*m.*) clock
el ray-*loh*

el rey (*m.*) king
el ray

el robot (*m.*) robot
el roh-*boht*

el sábado (*m.*) Saturday
el *sah*-bah-thoh

la semana (*f.*) week
lah say-*mah*-nah

la sirena (*f.*) mermaid
lah see-*ray*-nah

el sol (*m.*) sun
el sohl

el sombrero (*m.*) hat
el sohm-*bray*-roh

el tesoro (*m.*) treasure
el tay-*soh*-roh

la Tierra (*f.*) earth
lah tee-*ay*-rah

el tomate (*m.*) tomato
el toh-*mah*-tay

la torta (*f.*) pie; tart
lah *tohr*-tah

los uniformes (*m. pl.*) uniforms
lohs oo-nee-*fohr*-mays

la ventana (*f.*) window
lah bhayn-*tah*-nah

el verano (*m.*) summer
el bhay-*rah*-noh

el viernes (*m.*) Friday
el bhee-*ayr*-nays

el xilófono (*m.*) xylophone
el see-*loh*-foh-noh

el yate (*m.*) yacht
el *yah*-tay

la zanahoria (*f.*) carrot
lah sah-nah-*oh*-ree-ah

el zorro (*m.*) fox
el *soh*-roh

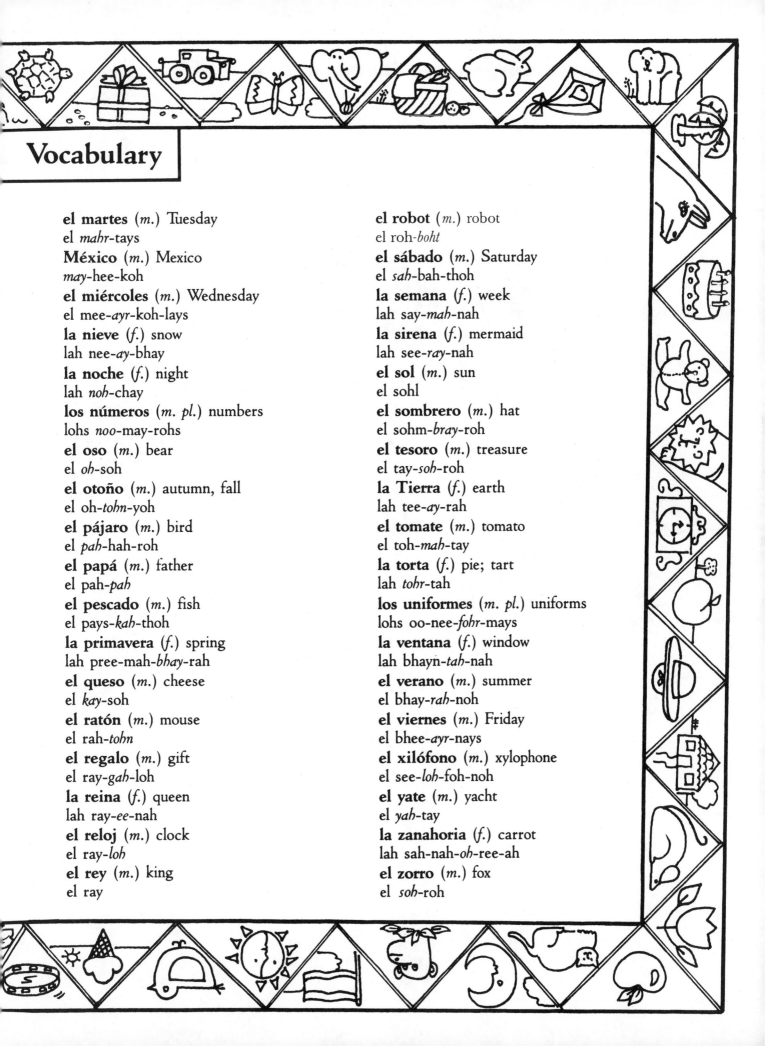

How Much Have You Learned?

Try to remember the Spanish word as you color each picture.